Starting and Ending

Your Week With the Holy Spirit

By Jeanetta Yeboah

Unless otherwise indicated, all scriptures are taken from King James Version (KJV) and New International Version (NIV).

Name of book: Starting and Ending Your Week With The Holy Spirit

ISBN: 1632270943

Copyright © 2015 by Jeanetta Yeboah

Publisher/Editor: Jeanetta Yeboah

Published by: Jeanetta Yeboah

P.O. Box 6171

Moreno Valley, CA 92554

About the Author

Jeanetta Yeboah is a human just like me and you. She had past experiences that she wasn't proud of. She battled with fear, depression, disappointments, and embedded concepts of religion. Things started to change on the first day that she decided to actively seek the face of the Lord for a personal revelation of who He was in her life. She was able to break free of her state of stagnancy and complacency, and she discovered a world of grace, new passions, new desires, and righteousness through the power of God.

God reached into her very heart and made a change. He broke down the walls that she had built around herself, and he replaced them with unconditional love and unique gifts. She was given the gift of intercessory prayer, praise & worship. She could now be a testimony of Christ to the world, and place Him above all other ideas and objections.

Every day, she continues to see the rewards of following God that have made themselves manifest in her life. Through this book, she is proud to invite you to join the path that God has created for you, and to develop your own relationship with Jesus. This woman is a testimony to everyone that she meets, and there is no doubt that she leaves a lasting impression on the hearts of everyone she encounters.

Table of Contents

Meditation is spending quality time with God. During this time, you are reviewing, reflecting and analyzing the word of God. After mediating on the word, application is needed. You must apply it. As you apply the word of God, you are allowing the Holy Spirit to reveal a vision for your personal life and then you capture what has been deposited. Many times we as Christians believe that we can meditate on the word without ever picking up the bible, and the word we think we know isn't quoted in the bible at all. Like, "God helps those who help themselves!" A lot of people really think that's in the bible, but its not. Therefore, we as believers need to get in our word so that we won't be deceived, misguided, but full of wisdom, and fruitful in everything that we do.

Meditating in the word is effective because when we go about living our every day life and circumstances arise, its that word that we speak that will change the situation. But if we don't know the word, the situation can't change. As Christians we should be meditating on the word, confessing the word, applying the word, and praising the Lord (with a sound mind) for manifestation of his word in our lives.

Many times as Christians we study a scripture for one day, only for the next day, never to reflect back on the scripture we learned. Which is a great illustration of our personal time with the Lord. Going to church once a week (or on Christmas, Mothers Day, or Easter) isn't enough. You have to set aside personal time with the Lord, in which you can study and mediate on his word. The bible declares in Joshua 1:8 "You shall meditate on it day and night, so that you may be careful to do according to all that is written in it; for then you will make your way prosperous, and then you will have success."By the end of this 52 week journal, your spirit will have absorbed 52 weeks of scriptures from the word of God. But don't stop there, this is just a stepping stone, continue your journey with the Lord, by getting in your word and finding new scriptures and meditating on them weekly.

I pray that you will be blessed as you meditate on the word of God. As you complete your Monday scripture, Tuesday-Sunday allow the Holy Spirit to speak into your spirit and write down every thing you hear as you go along. Therefore after completing this devotional when situations arise the word of God that you have studied will be brought to your remembrance by the Holy Spirit.

In addition to meditating on the scriptures for a victorious life, God wants you to draw closer to him during this process; in which he will draw hidden gifts and talents out of you. The key point, is that God wants you to draw closer to him, he is yearning for you to fellowship with him. As a result of fellowshipping with the Lord, he will: do a great work in your life, download new business ideas, heal your body, reconcile relationships, grant you divine wisdom. But all of this comes from being in direct fellowship with the Lord and walking in your rightful place as an heir of Christ.

Week # 1

Scripture of the week:

Proverbs 3:4 KJ

So shalt thou find favor and good understanding in the sight of God and man.

Luke 6:38 KJ

Give, and it shall be given unto you; good measure, pressed down, and shaken together, and running over, shall men give into your bosom.

Monday reflection from scripture

_____

_____

_____

_____

_____

_____

*Mediate on scriptures every day this week and write
down what the spirit shares with you.*

Tuesday

_____

_____

_____

Wednesday

_____

_____

_____

Thursday

_____

_____

_____

Friday

_____

_____

_____

Saturday

_____

_____

_____

Sunday

_____

_____

_____

Week #2

Scripture of the week:

Isaiah 58:11 NIV

The LORD will guide you always; he will satisfy your needs in a sun-scorched land and will strengthen your frame. You will be like a well-watered garden, like a spring whose waters never fail.

2 Corinthians 2:14 KJ

Now thanks be unto God, which always causeth us to triumph in Christ, and maketh manifest the savour of his knowledge by us in every place.

Monday reflection from scripture

_____

_____

_____

_____

_____

_____

*Mediate on scriptures every day this week and write
down what the spirit shares with you.*

Tuesday

_____

_____

Wednesday

_____

_____

Thursday

_____

_____

_____

Friday

_____

_____

_____

Saturday

_____

_____

_____

Sunday

_____

_____

_____

Week #3

Scripture of the week:

Jeremiah 32:40 NIV

I will make an everlasting covenant with them: I will never stop doing good to them, and I will inspire them to fear me, so that they will never turn away from me.

Proverbs 11:21 KJ

The seed of the righteous shall be delivered.

Monday reflection from scripture

_____

_____

_____

_____

_____

_____

Mediate on scriptures every day this week and write down what the spirit shares with you.

Tuesday

_____

_____

_____

Wednesday

_____

_____

_____

Thursday

_____

_____

_____

Friday

_____

_____

_____

Saturday

_____

_____

_____

Sunday

_____

_____

_____

Week# 4

Scripture of the week:

Proverbs 3:9 NIV

Honor the LORD with your wealth, with the first fruits of all your crops.

Mark 11:23 KJ

For verily I say unto you, That whosoever shall say unto this mountain, Be thou removed, and be thou cast into the sea; and shall not doubt in his heart, but shall believe that those things which he saith shall come to pass; he shall have whatsoever he saith.

Monday reflection from scripture

Mediate on scriptures every day this week and write down what the spirit shares with you.

Tuesday

Wednesday

Thursday

Friday

_____

_____

_____

Saturday

_____

_____

_____

Sunday

_____

_____

_____

Week # 5

Scripture of the week:

Isaiah 60:16 NLT

Powerful kings and mighty nations will satisfy your every need, as though you were a child nursing at the breast of a queen. You will know at last that I, the LORD, am your Savior and your Redeemer, the Mighty One of Israel.

Deuteronomy 8:18 KJ

But thou shalt remember the LORD thy God: for it is he that giveth thee power to get wealth.

Monday reflection from scripture

_____

_____

_____

_____

_____

_____

*Mediate on scriptures every day this week and write
down what the spirit shares with you.*

Tuesday

_____

_____

_____

Wednesday

_____

_____

_____

Thursday

_____

_____

_____

Friday

_____

_____

_____

Saturday

_____

_____

_____

Sunday

_____

_____

_____

Week # 6

Scripture of the week:

Psalm 46:1-3 NIV

God is our refuge and strength, an ever-present help in trouble. Therefore we will not fear, though the earth give way and the mountains fall into the heart of the sea, though its waters roar and foam and the mountains quake with their surging. There is a river whose streams make glad the city of God, the holy place where the Most High dwells.

Isaiah 41:10 NIV

So do not fear, for I am with you; do not be dismayed, for I am your God. I will strengthen you and help you; I will uphold you with my righteous right hand.

Monday reflection from scripture

_____

_____

_____

_____

_____

_____

*Mediate on scriptures every day this week and write
down what the spirit shares with you.*

Tuesday

_____

_____

_____

Wednesday

_____

_____

_____

Thursday

_____

_____

_____

Friday

_____

_____

_____

Saturday

_____

_____

_____

Sunday

_____

_____

_____

Week # 7

Scripture of the week:

Proverbs 11:25 KJ

The liberal soul shall be made fat: and he that watereth shall be watered also himself.

Romans 8:28 KJ

And we know that all things work together for good to them that love God, to them who are the called according to his purpose.

Monday reflection from scripture

_____

_____

_____

_____

_____

_____

Mediate on scriptures every day this week and write down what the spirit shares with you.

Tuesday

_____

_____

_____

Wednesday

_____

_____

_____

Thursday

_____

_____

_____

Friday

_____

_____

_____

Saturday

_____

_____

_____

Sunday

_____

_____

_____

Week #8

Scripture of the week:

Revelation 3:8 NIV

I know your deeds. See, I have placed before you an open door that no one can shut. I know that you have little strength, yet you have kept my word and have not denied my name.

Isaiah 54:17 KJ

No weapon that is formed against thee shall prosper; and every tongue that shall rise against thee in judgment thou shalt condemn. This is the heritage of the servants of the LORD, and their righteousness is of me, saith the LORD.

Monday reflection from scripture

_____

_____

_____

_____

_____

_____

*Mediate on scriptures every day this week and write
down what the spirit shares with you.*

Tuesday

_____

_____

Wednesday

_____

_____

Thursday

_____

_____

_____

Friday

_____

_____

_____

Saturday

_____

_____

_____

Sunday

_____

_____

_____

Week # 9

Scripture of the week:

Psalm 27:11 NLT

Teach me how to live, O LORD. Lead me along the right path, for my enemies are waiting for me.

Deuteronomy 28:7 NIV

The LORD will grant that the enemies who rise up against you will be defeated before you. They will come at you from one direction but flee from you in seven.

Monday reflection from scripture

_____

_____

_____

_____

_____

_____

*Mediate on scriptures every day this week and write
down what the spirit shares with you.*

Tuesday

_____

_____

_____

Wednesday

_____

_____

_____

Thursday

_____

_____

_____

Friday

_____

_____

_____

Saturday

_____

_____

_____

Sunday

_____

_____

_____

Week # 10

Scripture of the week:

Psalm 27:14 NLT

Wait patiently for the LORD. Be brave and courageous. Yes, wait patiently for the LORD.

Deuteronomy 28:3 KJ

Blessed shalt thou be in the city, and blessed shalt thou be in the field.

Monday reflection from scripture

_____

_____

_____

_____

_____

_____

*Mediate on scriptures every day this week and write
down what the spirit shares with you.*

Tuesday

_____

_____

Wednesday

_____

_____

Thursday

_____

_____

_____

Friday

_____

_____

_____

Saturday

_____

_____

_____

Sunday

_____

_____

_____

Week # 11

Scripture of the week:

Titus 2:12 NIV

For the grace of God has appeared that offers salvation to all people. It teaches us to say "No" to ungodliness and worldly passions, and to live self-controlled, upright and godly lives in this present age.

Proverbs 1:7 NIV

The fear of the LORD is the beginning of knowledge, but fools despise wisdom and instruction.

Monday reflection from scripture

_____

_____

_____

_____

_____

_____

*Mediate on scriptures every day this week and write
down what the spirit shares with you.*

Tuesday

_____

_____

_____

Wednesday

_____

_____

_____

Thursday

_____

_____

_____

Friday

_____

_____

_____

Saturday

_____

_____

_____

Sunday

_____

_____

_____

Week # 12

Scripture of the week:

John 15:7 KJ

If ye abide in me, and my words abide in you, ye shall ask what ye will, and it shall be done unto you.

Joshua 1:3 KJ

Every place that the sole of your foot shall tread upon, that have I given unto you, as I said unto Moses.

Monday reflection from scripture

_____

_____

_____

_____

_____

_____

*Mediate on scriptures every day this week and write
down what the spirit shares with you.*

Tuesday

_____

_____

_____

Wednesday

_____

_____

_____

Thursday

_____

_____

_____

Friday

_____

_____

_____

Saturday

_____

_____

_____

Sunday

_____

_____

_____

Week # 13

Scripture of the week:

Acts 17:28 NLT

For in him we live and move and exist.

Psalm 24:7-10 KJ

Lift up your heads, O ye gates; and be ye lift up, ye everlasting doors; and the King of glory shall come in. Who is this King of glory? The Lord strong and mighty, the Lord mighty in battle. Lift up your heads, O ye gates; even lift them up, ye everlasting doors; and the King of glory shall come in. Who is this King of glory? The Lord of hosts, he is the King of glory. Selah.

Monday reflection from scripture

_____

_____

_____

_____

_____

_____

*Mediate on scriptures every day this week and write
down what the spirit shares with you.*

Tuesday

_____

_____

_____

Wednesday

_____

_____

_____

Thursday

_____

_____

_____

Friday

_____

_____

_____

Saturday

_____

_____

_____

Sunday

_____

_____

_____

Week # 14

Scripture of the week:

Psalm 28:7 NIV

The LORD is my strength and my shield; my heart trusts in him, and he helps me. My heart leaps for joy, and with my song I praise him.

Psalm 68:1 KJ

Let God arise, let his enemies be scattered:

Monday reflection from scripture

_____

_____

_____

_____

_____

_____

_____

_____

*Mediate on scriptures every day this week and write
down what the spirit shares with you.*

Tuesday

_____

_____

_____

Wednesday

_____

_____

_____

Thursday

_____

_____

_____

Friday

_____

_____

_____

Saturday

_____

_____

_____

Sunday

_____

_____

_____

Week # 15

Scripture of the week:

Psalm 97:5 NIV

The mountains melt like wax before the LORD, before the Lord of all the earth.

Deuteronomy 32:35 NIV

It is mine to avenge; I will repay. In due time their foot will slip; their day of disaster is near and their doom rushes upon them.

Monday reflection from scripture

_____

_____

_____

_____

_____

_____

*Mediate on scriptures every day this week and write
down what the spirit shares with you.*

Tuesday

_____

_____

_____

Wednesday

_____

_____

_____

Thursday

_____

_____

_____

Friday

Saturday

Sunday

Week # 16

Scripture of the week:

Psalm 91:10 NIV

No harm will overtake you, no disaster will come near your tent.

Romans 8:28 KJ

And we know that all things work together for good to them that love God, to them who are the called according to his purpose.

Monday reflection from scripture

_____
_____
_____
_____
_____
_____
_____
_____
_____

Mediate on scriptures every day this week and write down what the spirit shares with you.

Tuesday

_____
_____
_____

Wednesday

_____
_____
_____

Thursday

_____

_____

_____

Friday

_____

_____

_____

Saturday

_____

_____

_____

Sunday

_____

_____

_____

Week # 17

Scripture of the week:

Psalm 23:6 KJ

Surely goodness and mercy shall follow me all the days of my life: and I will dwell in the house of the LORD for ever

Philippians 4:19 KJ

But my God shall supply all your need according to his riches in glory by Christ Jesus.

Monday reflection from scripture

_____

_____

_____

_____

_____

_____

*Mediate on scriptures every day this week and write
down what the spirit shares with you.*

Tuesday

_____

_____

_____

Wednesday

_____

_____

_____

Thursday

_____

_____

_____

Friday

_____

_____

_____

Saturday

_____

_____

_____

Sunday

_____

_____

_____

Week # 18

Scripture of the week:

Psalm 84:11 KJ

For the LORD God is a sun and shield: the LORD will give grace and glory: no good thing will he withhold from them that walk uprightly.

Isaiah 59:1 KJ

Behold, the LORD'S hand is not shortened, that it cannot save; neither his ear heavy, that it cannot hear:

Monday reflection from scripture

_____

_____

_____

_____

_____

_____

*Mediate on scriptures every day this week and write
down what the spirit shares with you.*

Tuesday

_____

_____

_____

Wednesday

_____

_____

_____

Thursday

_____

_____

_____

Friday

_____

_____

_____

Saturday

_____

_____

_____

Sunday

_____

_____

_____

Week # 19

Scripture of the week:

Romans 5:19 NIV

For just as through the disobedience of the one man the many were made sinners, so also through the obedience of the one man the many will be made righteous.

Romans 5:1 KJ

Therefore being justified by faith, we have peace with God through our Lord Jesus Christ:

Monday reflection from scripture

_____

_____

_____

_____

_____

_____

*Mediate on scriptures every day this week and write
down what the spirit shares with you.*

Tuesday

_____

_____

_____

Wednesday

_____

_____

_____

Thursday

_____

_____

_____

Friday

_____

_____

_____

Saturday

_____

_____

_____

Sunday

_____

_____

_____

Week # 20

Scripture of the week:

John 15:5 NIV

I am the vine; you are the branches. If you remain in me and I in you, you will bear much fruit; apart from me you can do nothing.

John 14:16-17 KJ

And I will pray the Father, and he shall give you another Comforter, that he may abide with you for ever; Even the Spirit of truth; whom the world cannot receive, because it seeth him not, neither knoweth him: but ye know him; for he dwelleth with you, and shall be in you.

Monday reflection from scripture

_____

_____

_____

_____

_____

_____

*Mediate on scriptures every day this week and write
down what the spirit shares with you.*

Tuesday

_____

_____

Wednesday

_____

_____

Thursday

_____

_____

_____

Friday

_____

_____

_____

Saturday

_____

_____

_____

Sunday

_____

_____

_____

Week # 21

Scripture of the week:

Psalm 122:9 NIV

For the sake of the house of the LORD our God, I will seek your prosperity.

Matthew 9:29 KJ

According to your faith be it unto you.

Monday reflection from scripture

_____

_____

_____

_____

_____

_____

*Mediate on scriptures every day this week and write
down what the spirit shares with you.*

Tuesday

_____

_____

_____

Wednesday

_____

_____

_____

Thursday

_____

_____

_____

Friday

_____

_____

_____

Saturday

_____

_____

_____

Sunday

_____

_____

_____

Week # 22

Scripture of the week:

Psalm 91:7 NIV

A thousand may fall at your side, ten thousand at your right hand, but it will not come near you.

Numbers 23:23 KJ

Surely there is no enchantment against Jacob, neither is there any divination against Israel: according to this time it shall be said of Jacob and of Israel, What hath God wrought!

Monday reflection from scripture

_____

_____

_____

_____

_____

_____

*Mediate on scriptures every day this week and write
down what the spirit shares with you.*

Tuesday

_____

_____

_____

Wednesday

_____

_____

_____

Thursday

_____

_____

_____

Friday

_____

_____

_____

Saturday

_____

_____

_____

Sunday

_____

_____

_____

Week # 23

Scripture of the week:

2 Corinthians 5:17 KJ

Therefore if any man be in Christ, he is a new creature: old things are passed away; behold, all things are become new.

Philippians 3:13-14

Brethren, I count not myself to have apprehended: but this one thing I do, forgetting those things which are behind, and reaching forth unto those things which are before, I press toward the mark for the prize of the high calling of God in Christ Jesus.

Monday reflection from scripture

_____

_____

_____

_____

_____

_____

Mediate on scriptures every day this week and write down what the spirit shares with you.

Tuesday

_____

_____

_____

Wednesday

_____

_____

_____

Thursday

_____

_____

_____

Friday

_____

_____

_____

Saturday

_____

_____

_____

Sunday

_____

_____

_____

Week # 24

Scripture of the week:

Jeremiah 33:3 KJ

Call unto me, and I will answer thee, and shew thee great and mighty things, which thou knowest not.

Isaiah 25:7 KJ

And he will destroy in this mountain the face of the covering cast over all people, and the vail that is spread over all nations.

Monday reflection from scripture

_____

_____

_____

_____

_____

_____

_____

_____

*Mediate on scriptures every day this week and write
down what the spirit shares with you.*

Tuesday

_____

_____

_____

Wednesday

_____

_____

_____

Thursday

_____

_____

_____

Friday

_____

_____

_____

Saturday

_____

_____

_____

Sunday

_____

_____

_____

Week # 25

Scripture of the week:

Habakkuk 2:3 KJ

For the vision is yet for an appointed time, but at the end it shall speak, and not lie: though it tarry, wait for it; because it will surely come, it will not tarry.

Psalm 102:13 NIV

You will arise and have compassion on Zion, for it is time to show favor to her; the appointed time has come.

Monday reflection from scripture

_____

_____

_____

_____

_____

_____

*Mediate on scriptures every day this week and write
down what the spirit shares with you.*

Tuesday

_____

_____

_____

Wednesday

_____

_____

_____

Thursday

_____

_____

_____

Friday

Saturday

Sunday

Week # 26

Scripture of the week:

Deuteronomy 28:5 NIV

Your basket and your kneading trough will be blessed.

Deuteronomy 28:8 NIV

The LORD will send a blessing on your barns and on everything you put your hand to. The LORD your God will bless you in the land he is giving you.

Monday reflection from scripture

_____

_____

_____

_____

_____

_____

*Mediate on scriptures every day this week and write
down what the spirit shares with you.*

Tuesday

_____

_____

_____

Wednesday

_____

_____

_____

Thursday

_____

_____

_____

Friday

_____
_____
_____

Saturday

_____
_____
_____

Sunday

_____
_____
_____

Week # 27

Scripture of the week:

Ephesians 6:11

Put on the full armor of God, so that you can take your stand against the devil's schemes.

Ephesians 6:16 KJ

Above all, taking the shield of faith, wherewith ye shall be able to quench all the fiery darts of the wicked.

Monday reflection from scripture

_____

_____

_____

_____

_____

_____

_____

_____

Mediate on scriptures every day this week and write down what the spirit shares with you.

Tuesday

_____

_____

_____

Wednesday

_____

_____

_____

Thursday

_____

_____

_____

Friday

_____

_____

_____

Saturday

_____

_____

_____

Sunday

_____

_____

_____

Week # 28

Scripture of the week:

1 John 5:4 NIV

For everyone born of God overcomes the world. This is the victory that has overcome the world, even our faith.

Romans 12:2 KJ

And be not conformed to this world: but be ye transformed by the renewing of your mind, that ye may prove what is that good, and acceptable, and perfect, will of God.

Monday reflection from scripture

_____

_____

_____

_____

_____

_____

Mediate on scriptures every day this week and write down what the spirit shares with you.

Tuesday

_____

_____

_____

Wednesday

_____

_____

_____

Thursday

_____

_____

_____

Friday

_____
_____
_____

Saturday

_____
_____
_____

Sunday

_____
_____
_____

Week # 29

Scripture of the week:

Jeremiah 20:11 NIV

But the LORD is with me like a mighty warrior; so my persecutors will stumble and not prevail. They will fail and be thoroughly disgraced; their dishonor will never be forgotten.

Proverbs 26:27 NIV

Whoever digs a pit will fall into it; if someone rolls a stone, it will roll back on them.

Monday reflection from scripture

_____

_____

_____

_____

_____

_____

*Mediate on scriptures every day this week and write
down what the spirit shares with you.*

Tuesday

_____

_____

_____

Wednesday

_____

_____

_____

Thursday

_____

_____

_____

Friday

Saturday

Sunday

Week # 30

Scripture of the week:

Romans 4:17 KJ

(As it is written, I have made thee a father of many nations,) before him whom he believed, even God, who quickeneth the dead, and calleth those things which be not as though they were.

Romans 8:11 NIV

And if the Spirit of him who raised Jesus from the dead is living in you, he who raised Christ from the dead will also give life to your mortal bodies because of his Spirit who lives in you.

Monday reflection from scripture

_____

_____

_____

_____

_____

_____

*Mediate on scriptures every day this week and write
down what the spirit shares with you.*

Tuesday

_____

_____

_____

Wednesday

_____

_____

_____

Thursday

_____

_____

_____

Friday

_____

_____

_____

Saturday

_____

_____

_____

Sunday

_____

_____

_____

Week # 31

Scripture of the week:

Genesis 12:3 NIV

I will bless those who bless you, and whoever curses you I will curse; and all peoples on earth will be blessed through you."

Numbers 6:24-16 NIV

The Lord bless you and keep you; the Lord make his face shine on you and be gracious to you; the Lord turn his face toward you and give you peace.

Monday reflection from scripture

_____

_____

_____

_____

_____

_____

*Mediate on scriptures every day this week and write
down what the spirit shares with you.*

Tuesday

_____

_____

_____

Wednesday

_____

_____

_____

Thursday

_____

_____

_____

Friday

_____

_____

_____

Saturday

_____

_____

_____

Sunday

_____

_____

_____

Week # 32

Scripture of the week:

Genesis 1:28 KJ

And God blessed them, and God said unto them, Be fruitful, and multiply, and replenish the earth, and subdue it: and have dominion over the fish of the sea, and over the fowl of the air, and over every living thing that moveth upon the earth.

3 John 2:2 KJ

Beloved, I wish above all things that thou mayest prosper and be in health, even as thy soul prospereth.

Monday reflection from scripture

_____

_____

_____

_____

_____

_____

*Mediate on scriptures every day this week and write
down what the spirit shares with you.*

Tuesday

_____

_____

Wednesday

_____

_____

Thursday

_____

_____

_____

Friday

_____

_____

_____

Saturday

_____

_____

_____

Sunday

_____

_____

_____

Week # 33

Scripture of the week:

2 Corinthians 10:5 KJ

Casting down imaginations, and every high thing that exalteth itself against the knowledge of God, and bringing into captivity every thought to the obedience of Christ

Philippians 4:8 KJ

Finally, brethren, whatsoever things are true, whatsoever things are honest, whatsoever things are just, whatsoever things are pure, whatsoever things are lovely, whatsoever things are of good report; if there be any virtue, and if there be any praise, think on these things.

Monday reflection from scripture

_____

_____

_____

_____

_____

_____

*Mediate on scriptures every day this week and write
down what the spirit shares with you.*

Tuesday

_____

_____

_____

Wednesday

_____

_____

_____

Thursday

_____

_____

_____

Friday

_____

_____

_____

Saturday

_____

_____

_____

Sunday

_____

_____

_____

Week # 34

Scripture of the week:

Ephesians 6:12 KJ

For we wrestle not against flesh and blood, but against principalities, against powers, against the rulers of the darkness of this world, against spiritual wickedness in high places.

Luke 10:19 NIV

I have given you authority to trample on snakes and scorpions and to overcome all the power of the enemy; nothing will harm you.

Monday reflection from scripture

_____

_____

_____

_____

_____

_____

*Mediate on scriptures every day this week and write
down what the spirit shares with you.*

Tuesday

_____

_____

_____

Wednesday

_____

_____

_____

Thursday

_____

_____

_____

Friday

Saturday

Sunday

Week # 35

Scripture of the week:

Colossians 4:6 NIV

Let your conversation be always full of grace, seasoned with salt, so that you may know how to answer everyone.

Ecclesiastes 5:2 NIV

Do not be quick with your mouth, do not be hasty in your heart to utter anything before God. God is in heaven and you are on earth, so let your words be few.

Monday reflection from scripture

_____

_____

_____

_____

_____

_____

*Mediate on scriptures every day this week and write
down what the spirit shares with you.*

Tuesday

_____

_____

_____

Wednesday

_____

_____

_____

Thursday

_____

_____

_____

Friday

_____

_____

_____

Saturday

_____

_____

_____

Sunday

_____

_____

_____

Week # 36

Scripture of the week:

2 Corinithans 5:17 KJ

Therefore if any man be in Christ, he is a new creature: old things are passed away; behold, all things are become new.

2 Timothy 1:7 KJ

For God hath not given us the spirit of fear; but of power, and of love, and of a sound mind.

Monday reflection from scripture

_____

_____

_____

_____

_____

_____

Mediate on scriptures every day this week and write down what the spirit shares with you.

Tuesday

_____

_____

_____

Wednesday

_____

_____

_____

Thursday

_____

_____

_____

Friday

_____

_____

_____

Saturday

_____

_____

_____

Sunday

_____

_____

_____

Week # 37

Scripture of the week:

Psalm 1:3 KJ

And he shall be like a tree planted by the rivers of water, that bringeth forth his fruit in his season; his leaf also shall not wither; and whatsoever he doeth shall prosper.

Hebrews 4:12 NIV

For the word of God is alive and active. Sharper than any double-edged sword, it penetrates even to dividing soul and spirit, joints and marrow; it judges the thoughts and attitudes of the heart.

Monday reflection from scripture

_____

_____

_____

_____

_____

_____

*Mediate on scriptures every day this week and write
down what the spirit shares with you.*

Tuesday

_____

_____

_____

Wednesday

_____

_____

_____

Thursday

_____

_____

_____

Friday

_____

_____

_____

Saturday

_____

_____

_____

Sunday

_____

_____

_____

Week # 38

Scripture of the week:

Luke 3:5 KJ

Every valley shall be filled, and every mountain and hill shall be brought low; and the crooked shall be made straight, and the rough ways shall be made smooth.

Isaiah 43:15-19 NIV

I am the Lord, your Holy One, Israel's Creator, your King. This is what the Lord says—he who made a way through the sea, a path through the mighty waters, who drew out the chariots and horses, the army and reinforcements together, and they lay there, never to rise again, extinguished, snuffed out like a wick: Forget the former things; do not dwell on the past. See, I am doing a new thing! Now it springs up; do you not perceive it? I am making a way in the wilderness and streams in the wasteland.

Monday reflection from scripture

_____
_____
_____

_____
_____
_____

*Mediate on scriptures every day this week and write
down what the spirit shares with you.*

Tuesday

_____
_____
_____

Wednesday

_____
_____
_____

Thursday

_____
_____
_____

Friday

_____
_____
_____

Saturday

_____
_____
_____

Sunday

_____
_____
_____

Week # 39

Scripture of the week:

Matthew 18:18 KJ

Verily I say unto you, Whatsoever ye shall bind on earth shall be bound in heaven: and whatsoever ye shall loose on earth shall be loosed in heaven.

Matthew 11:12 KJ

And from the days of John the Baptist until now the kingdom of heaven suffereth violence, and the violent take it by force.

Monday reflection from scripture

_____

_____

_____

_____

_____

_____

*Mediate on scriptures every day this week and write
down what the spirit shares with you.*

Tuesday

_____

_____

_____

Wednesday

_____

_____

_____

Thursday

_____

_____

_____

Friday

Saturday

Sunday

Week # 40

Scripture of the week:

2 Corinthians 4:16 KJ

For which cause we faint not; but though our outward man perish, yet the inward man is renewed day by day.

John 14:26 NIV

But the Advocate, the Holy Spirit, whom the Father will send in my name, will teach you all things and will remind you of everything I have said to you.

Monday reflection from scripture

_____

_____

_____

_____

_____

_____

*Mediate on scriptures every day this week and write
down what the spirit shares with you.*

Tuesday

_____

_____

_____

Wednesday

_____

_____

_____

Thursday

_____

_____

_____

Friday

_____

_____

_____

Saturday

_____

_____

_____

Sunday

_____

_____

_____

Week # 41

Scripture of the week:

Hebrews 11:1 KJ

Now faith is the substance of things hoped for, the evidence of things not seen.

James 2:17 NIV

In the same way, faith by itself, if it is not accompanied by action, is dead.

Monday reflection from scripture

_____

_____

_____

_____

_____

_____

_____

_____

_____

Mediate on scriptures every day this week and write down what the spirit shares with you.

Tuesday

_____

_____

_____

Wednesday

_____

_____

_____

Thursday

Friday

Saturday

Sunday

Week # 42

Scripture of the week:

James 1:8 KJ

A double minded man is unstable in all his ways.

Proverbs 3:6 KJ

In all thy ways acknowledge him, and he shall direct thy paths.

Monday reflection from scripture

_____

_____

_____

_____

_____

_____

_____

_____

_____

Mediate on scriptures every day this week and write down what the spirit shares with you.

Tuesday

_____

_____

_____

Wednesday

_____

_____

_____

Thursday

Friday

Saturday

Sunday

Week # 43

Scripture of the week:

Hebrews 10:23 KJ

Let us hold fast the profession of our faith without wavering; (for he is faithful that promised.)

Isaiah 55:11 KJ

So shall my word be that goeth forth out of my mouth: it shall not return unto me void, but it shall accomplish that which I please, and it shall prosperin the thing whereto I sent it.

Monday reflection from scripture

_____

_____

_____

_____

_____

_____

*Mediate on scriptures every day this week and write
down what the spirit shares with you.*

Tuesday

_____

_____

_____

Wednesday

_____

_____

_____

Thursday

_____

_____

_____

Friday

_____

_____

_____

Saturday

_____

_____

_____

Sunday

_____

_____

_____

Week # 44

Scripture of the week:

Proverbs 18:21 KJ

Death and life are in the power of the tongue: and they that love it shall eat the fruit thereof.

Luke 6:45 NIV

A good man brings good things out of the good stored up in his heart, and an evil man brings evil things out of the evil stored up in his heart. For the mouth speaks what the heart is full of.

Monday reflection from scripture

_____

_____

_____

_____

_____

_____

_____

_____

_____

*Mediate on scriptures every day this week and write
down what the spirit shares with you.*

Tuesday

_____

_____

_____

Wednesday

_____

_____

_____

Thursday

_____

_____

_____

Friday

_____

_____

_____

Saturday

_____

_____

_____

Sunday

_____

_____

_____

Week # 45

Scripture of the week:

Isaiah 53:5 KJ

But he was wounded for our transgressions, he was bruised for our iniquities: the chastisement of our peace was upon him; and with his stripes we are healed.

Malachi 4:2 NLT

But for you who fear my name, the Sun of Righteousness will rise with healing in his wings. And you will go free, leaping with joy like calves let out to pasture.

Monday reflection from scripture

_____

_____

_____

_____

_____

_____

*Mediate on scriptures every day this week and write
down what the spirit shares with you.*

Tuesday

_____

_____

_____

Wednesday

_____

_____

_____

Thursday

_____

_____

_____

Friday

Saturday

Sunday

Week # 46

Scripture of the week:

1 Corinthians 2:12 NIV

What we have received is not the spirit of the world, but the Spirit who is from God, so that we may understand what God has freely given us.

John 10:10 KJ

I am come that they might have life, and that they might have it more abundantly.

Monday reflection from scripture

_____

_____

_____

_____

_____

_____

*Mediate on scriptures every day this week and write
down what the spirit shares with you.*

Tuesday

_____

_____

_____

Wednesday

_____

_____

_____

Thursday

_____

_____

_____

Friday

___

Saturday

___

Sunday

___

Week # 47

Scripture of the week:

2 Corinthians 5:21 KJ

For he hath made him to be sin for us, who knew no sin; that we might be made the righteousness of God in him.

Romans 10:4 ESV

For Christ is the end of the law for righteousness to everyone who believes.

Monday reflection from scripture

_____

_____

_____

_____

_____

_____

_____

_____

_____

*Mediate on scriptures every day this week and write
down what the spirit shares with you.*

Tuesday

_____

_____

_____

Wednesday

_____

_____

_____

Thursday

_____

_____

_____

Friday

_____

_____

_____

Saturday

_____

_____

_____

Sunday

_____

_____

_____

Week # 48

Scripture of the week:

Proverbs 2:6 NIV

For the LORD gives wisdom; from his mouth come knowledge and understanding.

James 1:5 NIV

If any of you lacks wisdom, you should ask God, who gives generously to all without finding fault, and it will be given to you.

Monday reflection from scripture

_____

_____

_____

_____

_____

_____

_____

_____

_____

Mediate on scriptures every day this week and write down what the spirit shares with you.

Tuesday

_____

_____

_____

Wednesday

_____

_____

_____

Thursday

_____
_____
_____

Friday

_____
_____
_____

Saturday

_____
_____
_____

Sunday

_____
_____
_____

Week # 49

Scripture of the week:

James 5:16 NIV

The prayer of a righteous person is powerful and effective.

Luke 1:45 KJ

And blessed is she that believed: for there shall be a performance of those things which were told her from the Lord.

Monday reflection from scripture

_____

_____

_____

_____

_____

_____

_____

_____

Mediate on scriptures every day this week and write down what the spirit shares with you.

Tuesday

_____

_____

_____

Wednesday

_____

_____

_____

Thursday

Friday

Saturday

Sunday

Week # 50

Scripture of the week:

Philippians 4:6-7 KJ

Be anxious for nothing, but in everything by prayer and supplication, with thanksgiving, let your requests be made known to God; and the peace of God, which surpasses all understanding, will guard your hearts and minds through Christ Jesus.

Psalm 138:8 KJ

The Lord will perfect that which concerneth me.

Monday reflection from scripture

_____

_____

_____

_____

_____

_____

*Mediate on scriptures every day this week and write
down what the spirit shares with you.*

Tuesday

_____

_____

_____

Wednesday

_____

_____

_____

Thursday

_____

_____

_____

Friday

_____

_____

_____

Saturday

_____

_____

_____

Sunday

_____

_____

_____

Week # 51

Scripture of the week:

Colossians 2:8 KJ

Beware lest any man spoil you through philosophy and vain deceit, after the tradition of men, after the rudiments of the world, and not after Christ.

Mark 7:13 NIV

Thus you nullify the word of God by your tradition that you have handed down. And you do many things like that.

Monday reflection from scripture

_____

_____

_____

_____

_____

_____

*Mediate on scriptures every day this week and write
down what the spirit shares with you.*

Tuesday

_____

_____

_____

Wednesday

_____

_____

_____

Thursday

_____

_____

_____

Friday

_____

_____

_____

Saturday

_____

_____

_____

Sunday

_____

_____

_____

Week # 52

Scripture of the week:

John 4:13-14 KJ

Jesus answered and said unto her, Whosoever drinketh of this water shall thirst again: But whosoever drinketh of the water that I shall give him shall never thirst; but the water that I shall give him shall be in him a well of water springing up into everlasting life.

Genesis 8:22 NIV

As long as the earth endures, seedtime and harvest, cold and heat, summer and winter, day and night will never cease.

Monday reflection from scripture

_____

_____

_____

_____

_____

_____

*Mediate on scriptures every day this week and write
down what the spirit shares with you.*

Tuesday

_____

_____

Wednesday

_____

_____

Thursday

_____

_____

_____

Friday

_____

_____

_____

Saturday

_____

_____

_____

Sunday

_____

_____

_____

Bibles References

Amplified (AMP)

English Standard Version (ESV)

King James (KJ)

New American Standard Bible (NASB)

New International Version (NIV)

New Literal Translation (NLT)

Website: www.Jeanettayeboah.com

Other books:

Grace of God, Righteousness For Your Situation

Conversations with God